VISIONS REVISITED

Visions Revisited

Sherry Preston

Library of Congress Control Number: 2011916065
ISBN: Hardcover   978-1-4653-6301-5
               Softcover   978-1-4653-6300-8
               Ebook   978-1-4653-6302-2

This book was printed in the United States of America.

To order additional copies of this book, contact:
Xlibris Corporation
1-888-795-4274
www.Xlibris.com
Orders@Xlibris.com
82795

Contents

The Hunt That Got My Goat

One of the most unforgettable hunts I ever went on was for mountain goats on the mainland many miles from home. My father, his two business partners, and a thirteen-year-old boy headed to a remote lake for what we thought would be a two-day trip. The first day was beautiful—we set up our camp on the lakeshore then climbed the cliffs nearby to hunt. We immediately spotted three goats and split up to chase them. I went to the top of the cliff and saw two of the goats running by below me. There was no chance to shoot, but as they ran out of sight behind the rocks, I heard two shots. My father had gone over the cliff top and down the other side, and the goats passed right by him (or tried to). The third goat was between the cliff and the lake and didn't get past the other three hunters. We were in high spirits that night, with three success stories to brag about when we got home, but the euphoria ended early the next morning. A storm had moved in, and we spent the next six days trying to stop the leaks in the tent or just trying to keep it from being blown away. There was also a shortage of food as we hadn't planned on such a long stay. I had never eaten goat before, and I certainly hope I never get a second chance—that meat was very tough and far from tasty, but at least we weren't going to starve.

Day seven finally arrived, and there was a break in the storm just long enough for a seaplane to fly in and pick us up one at a time. We left the tent behind, and as far as I know, it has never been retrieved.

Trapping

I had many experiences with wildlife since the whole family hunted, fished, and trapped. Trapping, in particular, was guaranteed to produce some close encounters. There was sure to be a fight waiting at every trap we checked since our traplines targeted mink, marten, and attar—three of the most vicious species around. I remember one exceptionally angry marten that I had to deal with. I usually used a club to subdue an animal, but this time I had nothing available, so I used my fist. I had no idea an animal could move so fast—every time I tried to hit it, it dodged and bit at the same time. I finally managed to connect by swinging both fists, and it was over, finally. I had seventeen bites on one hand and two on the other to remember that little rascal by. He ended up as part of a fun hat, which I still have.

Otters were not only mean, they were smart too. I saw, several times, indications that they carried rocks up from the beach and used them to trip the traps we set. We countered that by setting two traps, which had a 75 percent success rate. Even then, those sneaky otters managed to avoid getting caught. My favorite method was to wait near their dens, and after they went in, I would place at least four traps in front and then go back to waiting. My success rate was much improved, although I still had to deal with a very angry animal that was stronger than I was. There were times when I took the safest course and shot them, although it damaged the fur.

My most memorable encounter came when I saw an otter crossing a small pond one day. I had an old small-caliber rifle with me, and I shot just as he climbed up on the bank. One big splash, and—no otter. A minute later, I saw air bubbles coming my way, and then I saw the otter. He was just about to sink his teeth into my foot! My gun stock splintered when it hit his head, just hard enough to stun him, and then I shot him again. My father got quite a chuckle out of the story, and I got a new rifle that Christmas.

Pets

Growing up in one of the remote areas in Alaska was an endless adventure for me. My first clear memory was of a rather unique pet. It was a very young harbor seal, orphaned by hunters. Seals at the time were hunted regularly for a bounty, and thus the pup's mother was one of the casualties. It was so young that it had no teeth and really did not know how to swim well. My mother ground up clam meat and spoon-fed it until its teeth grew in, then she fed it fish. During this time, we discovered it was a male, and we named him Flipper. Over the next year, Flipper became a real attraction to the people in a nearby village, and he loved all the attention. He had learned his name and would come when we called. He also loved to jump high out of the water and splash anyone who was too close. He finally left to join other seals, and I have often wondered if he escaped the hunters. He was very smart, but also very friendly, and my fear is that he made himself an easy target.

My next pet of note was a young black-tailed deer about a year old. He appeared one winter when I was carrying water from a creek to the house. I had two pails with me, and I set them down while I chopped a hole in the ice. Having filled one pail, I started on the next pail. Suddenly, I heard a noise behind me and looked back to see a small deer drinking out of the first pail. He backed away when I turned around but followed me back to the house. I filled a third pail on my next trip to the creek and left it for him. The next day, he was waiting for me at the creek, and this time I took some vegetables along to give him: betters, carrots, and some cabbage leaves. He ate everything but the cabbage. And later on when other deer joined him, I noticed that they would not eat cabbage either. We eventually had thirteen deer coming to us for food and water, but that young deer and I were the best of friends all winter long. He would wait outside the front door for me every day, and we would go off into the forest to play. I tried hiding from him once, but he proved to be as good a tracker as any bloodhound. When he found me, he came and stood next to me and let me pet him for the first time. I will never forget the thrill of petting a wild deer!

When spring came, he left with the others, and I really missed him. All summer I watched the trees, hoping he would come back. Later that fall, he did come back, and I was surprised at the change in him. He was not the frisky yearling anymore, but a proved young buck with antlers, and he didn't stay long. I had the feeling he was both showing off and saying a final good-bye since I never saw him again. We told other hunters for the next few years that there were no deer in the area, in an effort to keep our herd safe. My father and brothers went miles away to do their hunting to keep up the pretense, and to the best of my knowledge, it worked. Two years later, I saw one of the other deer, a huge buck now in his prime, and he remembered us too. He came right to the house and got his special treat, which was a bar of chocolate, then left as quickly as he came. We moved soon after and took a lot of memories with us

Bears, Anyone?

Bears were numerous wherever I lived in those days, and it was inevitable that I would have some encounters. Once I discovered that I could actually scare them, the game was on. I fought over berry fishes with them, chased them away from my fish, and even treed one in the backyard. There were some special meetings along the way though.

My first bicycle was my pride and joy, and I couldn't wait to try it out on a nearby road. I left it there while I went home to pack bunch and returned to find that a bear had chewed up the seat and flattened both tires. Unfortunately for him, he was still in the area, and I went after him with all rage I could muster as well as every big rock I could find. We were many yards down the road before he began to autumn me. If he had stopped to fight, I would have welcomed it at that point.

Later on, I met a tame bear for the first time. Although he roamed free, he was very friendly, and the local flocks called him Sam. Sam was about three years old, and one leg showed signs of past injury as he walked with a limp. After I took food scraps over to where he was frequently seen, he would come when I called his name and eat from my hand. His mother also showed up there at times, although she had two tiny cubs, and I stayed out of her way

Bear number three was definitely the most comical meeting of all. I had been watching it feeding along the beach for a while, and I decided to take my boat over there and walk up for a closer look. I crouched low in the tall grass and watched for a few minutes until the bear suddenly looked up then charged! I immediately jumped up, flung my coat wide-open, and yelled loudly. That bear screeched to a halt, and I could almost hear him thinking, "What do I do now?" This expression was really priceless; I've never since seen shock on a bear's face. I began to back away, but after I had gone a few feet, he charged again. I did the coat-flap again, and this time, I huffed like a bear. He turned around in his own length and ran like there was a wolf pack chasing him, and he left me laughing too hard to stand up. I have no intention of ever trying that again; next time, the bear might not stop. But I will always cherish the memory of the time I outbluffed a bear.

Local History

One of the things I most loved to do was explore the country around me. Many of the places I lived in were rich in history, and I and my family found a lot of interesting things. Mining was a major industry for years, and there were fourteen mines within ten miles of my home at one time before we moved to another job location. Prior to the mining days, that area was a crossroads for the native traders; in fact, the remains of a Russian trading post were within walking distance of the house, and we found numerous artifacts there. However, the best find was right next to us—we discovered a large cache of trade beads on a small peninsula just across from the old trading post. There were thousands of them; most were next to the ashes of a campfire, and some were buried under a large rock. It wasn't long before we had newspaper reporters and treasure hunters arriving to investigate, and of course, my mother seized the opportunity to keep everyone well fed.

Other points of interest were the mine buildings and ore heaps. I had become an avid rock collector by this time, and they were a never-ending source of supply. One unexpected discovery happened while I was searching for crabs at the mouth of a nearby river. I found the remains of an old sailing ship, which had carried gold ore from one of the mines. Research later identified the ship, but meanwhile, I had gathered quite a bit of ore and some of the hardware from the ship, such as copper pins that held the planks to the frame.

Some of the more unusual items were found by my father. He had stone ax heads, carved wooden boxes, old oil lamps, cones with Turkish uniting, and a piece of obsidian that someone had brought to trade for beads many years earlier.

We also made use of some of the old mining machines left behind. My father was an excelled machines, and he was able to repair an old tractor, which was put to good use in the business. Another project was an old steam locomotive, which had been bought by a collector. He hired us to transport it from the mine to a barge he had waiting. That job took almost a week and was frequently interrupted by the sight of one of the numerous old bottles scattered throughout the area. Nearly all were underground, but once a glint of glass peeped out, all work stopped and the digging began. I still have some of them, with interesting names like Mexican Mustang Liniment, Nuxated Iron, Davis Painkiller, etc. One in particular was Chris Morley, made by two bottlers in England. Years after finding it, my father met the granddaughter of one of the bottle makers! She was amazed that the bottle had travelled so far from home.

My personal treasure, found in a mine office building, was a stack of stock certificates that read "Territory of Alaska." These are now safely kept in a sealed clear envelope and only brought out once a year to check their condition. Nowadays, my walls and shelves are lined with memories, and I think it is time to tell their stories.

Fish Tales

I loved to fish, both in the ocean and in the rivers. My family spent almost every summer weekend fishing, and we rarely came home without a good catch. On one memorable trip, my mother caught a boatload with just one fish, a giant halibut. It was so big that it covered the entire bottom of the boat. Getting it into the boat was the work of three people. I estimated it to be about seven feet long and about three hundred pounds. We ate a lot of halibut that year! During the trip home, my father's sense of humor surfaced unexpectedly. My mother's feet were resting on the huge fish, and after a brief wink at me, he kicked the tail of the halibut to make it move, and mother went into a complete panic. She thought the fish was still alive, and she knew what one that big could do to a person, not to mention what it could do to a boat. She didn't speak to my father for days afterward.

A year or so later, I was fishing by myself and hooked a fish that I'm sure was even bigger, although I never was able to reel it in. I eventually had to cut the line. My father said I had hooked a rock, but as I told him, rocks don't swim or shake their heads.

Trout fishing was lots of fun too. The river nearby was a popular place, known even in Europe, as I discovered one day when I met a man from Germany, Usually though, I was the only one there, which gave me access to a treasure trove of lost lures. I often went up the river to fish, carrying only a small knife. With that, I would cut a branch from a tree, collect a length of fishing line from the hundreds of yards lying around, and choose a lure from the ones I had collected; then I would go fishing.

Many times, I came home with my limit of trout and hundreds of dollars worth of lures, which I repaired and added to the family's tackle boxes. The fish were usually smoked and stored in a freezer. One could choose from a selection of rainbow, cutthroat, and steelhead, as well as salmon during summer months. We also smoked halibut on occasion, although it was never a favorite. Sometimes fishing didn't require a lure. I learned that I could actually stalk and catch a fish with just my hands. On hot summer days, it was a double pleasure to cool off in the river and catch fish at the same time.

My Wild Youth

As a child, I loved to get up before sunrise and explore the cove where we lived. Most of the wildlife were active at night, and I had a lot of encounters with mink and attend. Usually, my parents were still asleep, so I didn't have school until 8:00 a.m. That gave me almost four to five hours to dig clams, chase crabs, fish, climb trees, or just sit and watch the world wake up; it was on one of those mornings that I met my first deer.

Behind our house was a small cove where I sat quite often watching for mink, and I had just seen one when movement across the cove caught my attention. A buck had just come out of the trees, and we stared at each other for a long moment before he started walking along the beach. I was excited at seeing something new to me, but that changed when I realized the buck was coming over to my side of the cove! The closer he got, the more nervous I got; and when he got within twenty feet, I felt fear building. By the time the deer reached me and sniffed my hat and the side of my head, I was totally petrified. It was only later that I realized this deer was just as nervous. Evidently he had not seen a human before and wanted to find out what I was.

The greatest surprise was yet to come—a year later, a buck became a frequent visitor to our garden and grew quite tame. I am almost certain it was the same deer.

Over the next three years, our buck became very famous—people from miles away were coming to meet him and take pictures. He loved all the attention and would even pose for the camera with his head up and displaying his antlers. One autumn, he showed up with a doe, and we named her Missy. She was delicate looking and shy; she never became as tame as he was but would still come to the garden with him. A few weeks later, two hunters came into our cove and shot both our deer. They were new to the area and had no idea these deer were tame. I was devastated, as was the rest of the family, but that was to be expected—all the folks in the region depended on deer meat as a large part of their food supply as we did. That winter, we received the final surprise—a young fawn appeared and quickly became part of the family. We fed him all winter, and he finally left us when the show melted. Nosey was, I'm sure, the son of our proud buck. And since his parents were killed, we took steps to make sure he didn't trust humans. It was hard to do, but we had to destroy his trust in us and make him wild again; we had to in order to make sure he survived. I guess it worked because we never saw him again.

In another location we had moved to, my deer education began it earnest. It was midwinter when deer began appearing on the beaches. They often did that when the snow was too deep in the woods for them to find food. I was the designated water carrier, and it was on one of my trips to the nearby creek. And it was there that I met a little buck who became one of my best friends. More deer joined him at the creek in the following days until we had twelve deer hanging around. They kept my father and me busy every day gathering food for them. Primary sources were Spanish moss and fresh cut red under branches. We stripped moss from every tree within a mile of the house, often climbing the trees to get the last strands. On one of these trips, we were both high in the trees when a big doe appeared and snatched one of the food sacks. I chased her for quite a distance before she dropped it. Once home, we divided the moss into piles for each deer. It was hard to keep control of that operation—twelve hungry deer can get quite vicious if they aren't kept apart while eating, and I was at the center of the dispute every day. Luckily, I was only struck once, but it hurt.

Deer number thirteen arrived a few weeks later and promptly became my second-best friend. She was the oldest deer any of us had ever seen; she was gray instead of brown, most of her teeth were gone, and the ones still there were loose. However, this little old doe had a very big personality, and with her at my side, mealtime became much more peaceful. She stood guard while I sorted the moss into thirteen equal piles, then ate her share. As the winter progressed, we discovered that they liked apples and most vegetables except cabbages. The old doe, who we named Frosty, had a love for chocolate and would do almost anything to get it. She would stand up and put her front feet on my father's shoulders in an attempt to snatch the candy out of his hands. We finally began opening candy bars before we went outside to avoid being mobbed. Our black cat got involved as well, often going out into the herd and breaking up their fights. All the deer were fascinated by him and would stop whatever they were doing to come over to him. I have photos of a small black cat surrounded by a dozen deer, all taking turns trying to sniff and even lick him.

The first little buck and I often went into the woods together to wander, and I was also watching him to learn more about what deer ate.

As spring approached, shoots and buds popped out everywhere, and again I watched the deer to see what they ate. They clearly favored alder buds, and I added that fact to my base of knowledge. Shortly after, all the deer left except Frosty. She stayed well into the spring, and we had begun to consider ways to take her with us when we relocated in the summer. She chose to go her own way before that time arrived, and I left there with memories of an experience that only comes once in a lifetime.

Wolf Tales

Before we moved to our trailer on land, my husband and I lived in a remote location, called Nossuk Bay. It was the source of many happy hours spent hunting, fishing, and picking plants and berries. There was a steady supply of wood for our stove, and life was a daily treat.

Nossuk Bay was quite large, with a sizeable stream and numerous small coves and islets. Bears, deer, geese, ducks, and the occasional mink were common sights. We discovered that the north side of the bay was on the local wolf pack's map—they came by once every two weeks. The first time they paid us a visit, it turned out to be one of my most memorable experiences and led to one of my favorite poems. The pack at that time had ten to fifteen members, but they sounded more like fifty due to the echoes. I never saw any after the first night but heard them often and saw their tracks. I know I was followed several times as I walked over to the stream to fish, but they were only curious. Wolves have been part of my life since I was very young, and I never had reason to fear them. I did, however, once have a chance to sing with a small pack, and it was magical! I was out hunting for a bear and, having seen a nice one, was making a stalk on it. Suddenly I saw a wolf run across an open area to my right, and my "wild side" took charge.

I howled long and loud and got an immediate response from not one, but several wolves. Two of them came back into the open area, and we began a chorus that lasted several minutes. The first wolf actually began to dance while he sang, something I had never seen before. His front paws were tapping the ground as if he were keeping a rhythm. I never saw the other wolves, but I think there were three of them. I forgot all about that bear and even forgot that I was carrying a rifle! I could easily have shot one of those wolves as they were only a hundred feet away, but the song and the memories were far more important.

Not-So-Great Storms

Sometimes the weather played a large part in our daily lives. Storms kept everyone indoors, especially the severe ones. I remember three in particular that actually changed the landscape and caused major damage throughout the area. They were given names such as the Good Friday Blow, the Thanksgiving Day Terror, and the Easter Blow. Each one left destruction on a wide scale.

Good Friday began as a usually calm morning. It was my turn to make breakfast, and I was almost done when I heard a distant roar. Next came the snapping sounds of hundreds of trees breaking as the first strong gust hit them. Within a minute, the trees around the house were also breaking and falling, and boards were being ripped off. Other trees were about to fall directly onto our house, and my father and I raced to put cables on them to try to keep them upright. We succeeded, but the aftermath left us all in disbelief. One tree had fallen across the tractor, three more had completely ripped off one side of the tool shed, and the trees my father had meant to harvest were nearly all destroyed. Wind speed was later claimed to be in excess of one hundred miles per hour. This was just the beginning of what evolved into a legend.

We usually invited neighbors over for Thanksgiving dinner, and there were about eight people that day helping prepare the meal. Suddenly, we noticed how quiet the surrounding forest was—no birds, no breeze, just deep silence. Then we all heard that distant roar. This time, it not only blew down a lot of trees, it also sank two of our three boats. The neighbors lost one of their boats as well.

Easter Sunday was a lovely day at first. A huge spread across the sky in the afternoon, but everything looked normal otherwise. My father was gone on a business trip to Ketchikan, so my mother and I worked on our various hobbies. It was nearly midnight when I went to check our barometer, and the needle dropped down farther than I had ever seen it go before. I only had time to turn and look at my mother before the first gust hit and blew our back door off the hinges and right into the living room. From then on, it was complete chaos. We were living on a sort of houseboat at the time, and all the mooning lines broke at once. We were being blown toward a rocky beach, but I was able to use my own boat to steer everything to a small stretch of sand. Then I decided to try to reach our nearest neighbors in the next cove. That was one of the most frightening boat rides I had ever taken, with extremely high winds and waves to match. I succeeded though, and they came back with me to help watch over things. This storm also hit elsewhere, knocking over the radio tower in Ketchikan, blowing down trees on a scale no one had ever seen before, and completely destroying a freight facility. The anemometer at the weather station registered sustained winds of over two hundred miles an hour.

All those storms came from the southwest, and even to this day, I still shudder when the weather report calls for a southwest wind!

Weather "Science"

The art of weather prediction has been evolving for centuries but, even with all the present technology, still cannot be considered as accurate. On the other hand, people who live in rural or wilderness areas seem to have a higher percentage of accuracy in forecasting the weather than scientists do. I have seen this countless times and even made a few successful predictions myself. These people have learned to read the signs in nature that point to imminent weather changes, such as unnatural calm, wind direction, and even the appearance and action of certain plants and animals. For instance, I remember that the worst storms were always preceded by an eerie silence—no birds could be heard, and the air seemed to be almost stagnant. Other signs of approaching storms were found in trees such as alder; the leaves would turn over, exposing their bottom sides to the sky, when rain was on the way. Also, whenever sea gulls take baths or fly in high circles, count on gale-force winds within twenty-four hours!

Long-term predictions were also based on the flora and fauna. When deer and bears begin to grow their winter coats and the leaves changes color early, look for a long, cold winter. There are many other indications, but the folks who see and understand them are nearly 100 percent accurate in their forecasts!

Medical Mishaps

Part of living as I do in this rural/wild area is being able to deal with accidents and medical problems. To that end, I began taking emergency medical training and joined an ambulance squad. There have been some memorable times since; the lifestyle and occupations of the local folks generate some truly exciting calls for help. For instance, there was the man with chest pain on a fishing boat some distance from shore. Two of us got a ride out to meet his boat and bring him back to the clinic. We had transferred our patient to the rescue boat and were on the way back when we encountered rough water. The first wave caused an unexpected crisis—the man's heart, which had been beating too fast, suddenly stopped just long enough to throw me and my partner into a panic; then it started again at a normal rate. Technology has given the medical profession many excellent devices for saving lives, and I have used some of them, but I've yet to see a cardiac machine as effective as one ocean wave was that night! The second most memorable call was for a young man having seizures. Again, only two of us responded, along with a local police officer. I, being the senior medic, took the bad and was checking the patient with the help of his coworkers when he abruptly erupted into another seizure. We actually had to jump out of the way—he went airborne, screaming, and was spinning around, kicking at everyone. Once he stopped, six of us moved in and secured him to a wheeled cot for transport to the clinic. He was my fourth woo lent patient, and since I would be alone with him on the trip, I began to check all the restraints again and suddenly realized he was not breathing! My first thought was to call to my partner, who was driving, and tell him to hurry; then I began to perform CPR on the boy. Happily, I was able to revive him in just over a minute, and by then, we arrived at the clinic and the doctors took over. The young man recovered and went home, but the thrill of actually saving a life will never leave me. My partner and I were part of a miracle that night, and I'll tell the world all our lives were brightened because of it.

All ambulance calls were not so serious—we had our fair share of comedy too. I recall the youngster one winter who took his sled up on the roof of his house with the idea of getting a longer and faster ride down the hill below. He was stopped short by the icy ridge at the edge of the roof, which caused him to fly through the air and land on the road. Fortunately, he was wearing thick clothing, and the snow was deep enough to provide a cushion. We arrived to find a very scared child and a hysterical mother. Most of our treatment was trying to soothe jangled nerves, and in the end, all the boy had were some bruises and an increased respect for the laws of gravity, and we had another story to tell at the monthly meetings.

Shopping, Alaska Style

My husband and I often bought gifts for each other that were meant as jokes. He would bring home such things as pens with strings attached because I was constantly searching for pens. I got him bright-orange hats so he could always find one instead of looking everywhere.

One of his jokes was turned back on him at last. Our anniversary was a week away when he came home—with a set of reloading dies. (Reloading dies are used in the process of making ammunition at home instead of buying it.) Imagine his surprise when I started using them to load my own ammunition! I became quite good at it during the next few years. One of the highlights of that period was the time I was just finishing the loading of some rifle cases, when I looked out the window and saw a big black bear walking by. The window was the kind that would slide open, so I loaded my rifle, opened the window, and using the table as a rest, shot the bear. It proved to be a fat six-foot-long bear, and it was too heavy for me to move without help, so I skinned and quartered it on the spot. That bear provided two hundred pounds of meat, a good "shopping" trip indeed. I know of no other way to get so much good meat for forty cents—the price of one bullet.

Wild Bounty

One spring, my husband and I met two bean hunters who were looking for a nice trophy bean apiece. They were also looking for a place to stay, and we had a small cabin next to out trailer; so they stayed there for four days, and I cooked dinner every night for all of us. They quickly got used to my "government recipes," which consisted of wild game and plants we gathered. One of the hunters (who happened to be an outdoor writer) said he had never tasted better food than my crab stir-fry with wild ferns and mushrooms, a salad of other wild greens, as well as steamed wild asparagus with clam sauce. Dessert was a serving of biscuits topped with thimble berry jam from the fall of the previous year. Each night's dinner was different as I wanted to give them a good variety. We ate pizza with fresh bean meat from one of the trophies they got and another salad with different greens. And there were shrimp fritters and oysters bath fried and stewed; and for snacks, I introduced them to venison jerky, smoked salmon, and kelp pickles. They also experienced wild licorice, seaweed snacks, and tea made from leaves I had gathered and dried. In four days, they never once ate something from a store, and in the years since, they both still talked about the experience of living off the land as I and my husband did. One of the hunters came back several times to stay with us while he hunted. One autumn, I took him fishing and showed him my method of catching salmon by hand. I often waited in a shallow stream for fish to swim by; then one quick grab was all it took to catch one by the tail and throw it to the shore. I could usually catch my daily limit without using any fishing gear at all. My friend eventually caught a small fish, and we had fresh steamed salmon steaks that night along with a nice white wine he had brought with him.

I had a lifelong interest in the plants and wildlife of my world and all their uses. One could live a very healthy life by gathering the various plants, mushrooms, and fruits available. Besides their food value, they had medicinal properties, and some even had cosmetic applications. Certain trees provided more than lumber and firewood; their inner bark could be eaten and even woven into baskets and clothing. Sap from some trees could be used as glue, and their cones had seeds that tasted much like walnuts. In short, we could live very well without even going to others to buy food, and I did just that for many years.

Fun and Games

At an early age, I was introduced to the world of card games. Canasta, pinochle, hearts, and cribbage were nightly events at our house, and I soon discovered a love for cribbage in particular. I became so good at it that I even played for money in later years. There was a man who claimed to be the champion of southeast Alaska, and when he heard that I was also quite good, he came to visit us, and we played a set of three games. I won two and achieved the title of cribbage champion at age nine.

Where, Oh Where, Am I?

Travelling around this large island is always an adventure. Even though I grew up here, I have found more than once that it is very easy to get lost. I rescued myself twice, but the third time was quite a test of my survival skills.

I had taken the day to go hunting since it was between jobs, and the weather was nice for a change. I parked in a promising location and hiked up through a strip of trees to a high meadow to look for deer. Lots of trails were there, and I chose a fresh one and followed it down off the ridge and into more trees. After three hours of walking, I decided to head home. It was then I realized I had no idea which way to go. My compass was no help because, as I later discovered, that area was highly magnetic. I couldn't follow my tracks back because I hadn't made any. After assessing the situation, I headed for a large open area that I could see below my position and began building a shelter. It was a good location with freshwater nearby and lots of berries. I could see down the valley for nearly two miles, so I decided to stay there until I could determine where home was. One unnerving fact was the presence of some large bear tracks in the area, so I made camp a good distance from any berry patches.

Day two was rather nasty—the weather had changed, and no amount of work on the shelter could make it rainproof. I endured the second night soaking wet and shivering and was glad to see sunshine the next morning. That day, my third, was spent preparing signals for aircraft and eating every berry I could find. I had noticed that the searchers were all flying to and from one direction, so I had decided to head that way the next morning.

On the afternoon of day three, I saw a coast guard helicopter flying over the valley about a mile away, and I knew they could return the same way, so I made a flag to signal them when they flew past again. Sadly, the only suitable flag material was my underwear, so I sacrificed it. An hour later, the helicopter returned, and I waved my flag as hard as I could. It was a great relief to see them turn and come toward me! One stomach-churning ride later, I was back at my car where my husband was waiting along with two state troopers. They had been expecting someone who needed medical care and were prepared to transport, but I think I surprised them since I was quite healthy, apart from having numerous insect bites.

Now I never go hiking without a GPS and my cell phone, and I stay away from the temptation to follow game trails. My survival skills were sufficient, but I would rather not need them again.

The Ultimate Trapper

One of the job sites we moved to was close to a man who built boats most of the year and trapped wolves during the winter. Our two families quickly became friends, and I spent a lot of my spare time at his house, learning about wolves, and there was a vast store of information in that category! He also fished for salmon every summer, and my education grew to include the secrets of successful fishing and the various ways to catch, prepare, and preserve salmon. We enjoyed their company for three years until my father's fussiness took us elsewhere.

One of my favorite memories was made during Christmas at his house. We had planned a surprise for his two young sons, which involved a homemade sleigh and fells. I was enjoying watching the boys get excited thinking Santa was outside. They ran outside when their father called. Then my father pointed at me and said, "You too." I stepped outside—and there was a new boat in the yard with my name on it! At age fourteen, I started believing in Santa Claus again.

I often helped the neighbors with daily chores: shoveling snow, feeding their geese, etc. The geese were a domestic breed, and I soon found a good use for the term *birdbrain*. They loved to swim in the cove where he lived, and they could fly well—they just didn't know how to land! Many times I saw them simply fold their wings and fall twenty or thirty feet straight down to the water. Then there were the chickens, and they were far from being dumb. The day one rooster escaped became the definition of frustration for me. I spent most of a long afternoon chasing that feathered Houdini with no success. I finally gave up and left, having been completely outsmarted at every turn.

This trapper/boatbuilder had some truly amazing adventures with wolves. I actually saw him return home with live wolves in his boat! He would pick them up and carry them up to his shed, and they never tried to bite him. He said that once he tied their feet, they seemed to give up all attempts to escape. I suspect he kept one or two alive, because I later saw two of his dogs that looked very much like wolves.

To Cook or Not to Cook

Growing up in a logging camp made it difficult for my mother to teach me the homemaking arts. I was always helping my father with work or the equipment, and she refused to let me in the house at times until I washed all the grease off. I was nineteen before she saw me in a dress and then only because she promised me some money if I wore it. I knew more about fixing a broken-down engine than I did about cooking. Instead of sewing, I spliced cable, and I chopped more wood than vegetables. Eventually, she gave up trying and just let me follow my own interests. Oddly enough, I now enjoy cooking, sewing, and wearing nice clothes, but I also maintain a full toolbox and various power tools, and I love to do carpentry as well. Many times, instead of buying a shelf or a bookcase, I will study it then come home and build it myself. Knowing how to work on things has actually rescued me from some potentially dangerous situations over the years. It has also made me popular with some of my neighbors!

In short, I have become both my mother and father, and I can't think of a finer legacy.

Changing Times

My father operated a small logging business with my two older brothers, and I grew up while moving often from one logging site to the next. By the time I was fourteen, both brothers had left home. And against my mother's objections, I became a logger—to my knowledge, the only female logger in southeast Alaska. I held that job for twelve years and became very good at it. I was even hired by another logging camp one fall and replaced two in the process. I worked with my father on that job; we had become so attuned to each other that we functioned as a unit and ran a very smooth operation.

I truly enjoyed working in the woods every day, even in winter. It was a daily adventure. I never knew what might happen next! Neither did my mother; she always packed lunches for us and cleared the lunch pails every night. That stopped abruptly one evening when she opened mine and a bird flew out. From that point on, I opened it outside. The final straw came when she opened the storage box on the porch and a mink jumped out. I had strict orders from then on to bring home nothing but sandwich wrappers!

I was not the only one in the family who would do unexpected things. My father sometimes would suddenly stop work and follow a deer or an otter when it happened by, or just decide he would rather fish than work. My life during that twelve-year period was, to put it mildly, a series of good days, better days, and great days.

Eventually my father decided to sell his business and retire, and I was married soon after. It was the end of an idyllic life for me, an introduction to reality, and I miss those days still. Even though life has brought me many other delightful experiences, none can compare to those days when I lived and worked in one of the most wild and beautiful places on earth.

Water and Wood

Boats were a necessary thing in our lives. We each had our own boat, and then there was the family boat for hauling freight, towing logs to the lumber mill, or just taking cruises. There were no roads, so all traveling was done by boat or airplane. Small planes were everywhere, the kind that could land on water, and they were essential if one wanted mail delivery or freight that was needed immediately.

For my part, I was spending every spare minute on the water: fishing, exploring beaches, or just drifting with the wind. My parents placed a limit on how far I could go, but I seldom listened. That led to occasional groundings, but I was always straying as soon as they were lifted. On one jaunt, I went beyond the capacity of the fuel tank and realized I would have to row home, but I decided to explore first. Imagine my surprise when I found a container of the exact type of fuel I needed! I filled the tank and went home, and my parents never knew about my little adventure until I told them—years later.

Through this constant use of my boat and others, I became very good at maneuvering logs; and it won me a steady job with my father, working on the rafts as they were formed. (Rafts are a collection of logs held together inside a framework of other logs called boomsticks.) In my later years, these logs were gathered into bundles, wrapped with cables, and stored inside the framework. It was one of my jobs to use my boat to push or tow back a bundle into its proper place. When I was hired by another logging business with my father, that was what we did for six weeks, and I got the first paycheck of my young life—three thousand dollars. That was a huge amount for a teenager, but I didn't take long to spend it. My mother got a new washing machine, all the requirements for a complete bathroom, kitchen cabinets, and a new bed. She was very surprised and pleased that I had bought all these things for her instead of spending it on myself. I cherish to this day the joy she showed—it was worth far more to me than any amount of money.

Transitions

There was a period of thirteen years, after my father retired and I left home, that I spent in traveling through as many states as possible. Eventually, I visited forty states, as well as Canada and Mexico. I grew increasingly homesick for Alaska though, so I came home. On my first day back, I met the man I would soon marry. We dated for seven months then had a simple wedding. Twenty years later, I am alone, but those years were well spent as together we set out on a whole new series of adventures. My new husband lived far from the city and hunted and fished just like my family did, and I knew I had really come home when I moved in with him. We spent the first few years just living off the land then heard of a house for sale farther north. Since we were then living on a boat, moving was fairly easy (or so we thought). The move took more than a week, delayed by storms, time spent fishing for dinner, and a visit to one of my cousins. Upon arrival, we decided to explore the town nearby, where I overheard two people discussing "those two idiots" who came north with two boats in tow. Yes, we were notorious before we even arrived!

The house proved to be more than we had hoped for, and since it was built on a floating deck, we could stay wherever we chose and move when we got tired of the scenery. We spent eight years in this fashion and eventually ended up moving over eighty miles west with my brother's help. He towed the house float with his fishing boat to our new location. I soon took a temporary job operating a tiny country store when the owner was away buying supplies. When that job ended, another one arose at an oyster farm. I liked oysters, but by the time I left the farm, I couldn't stand looking at them! I had never realized how much work went into growing them, and I now have a deep respect for the people who farm them (even though I still won't eat any). We moved again, this time from the house to a small trailer on land. We found a nice place near a small lake, bought a truck from the oyster-farm owner, and began another chapter in our ever-changing life story. Three years later, we met a man who was out there checking his wolf traps. It wasn't long before he asked me to come work for him. He was a taxidermist and needed someone to help with the processing of furs brought in during the spring hunting season. I worked there for five years and learned a lot. During this time, my husband and I moved to the city, where I still live, and finally abandoned our nomadic life. In the sixth year, I opened my own taxidermy shop and had moderate success. I still do that work but have also become involved in the local emergency service and other social programs.

My husband of twenty happy years lost his fight with cancer this year, and it strengthened my determination to expand my medical training so I could help more. I have discovered though that quite often, a sympathetic ear and a warm shoulder can help more than a handful of pills, and I can offer both.

www.ingramcontent.com/pod-product-compliance
Lightning Source LLC
Chambersburg PA
CBHW061227280526
45784CB00006B/2668